CELTIC RECIPES

Sian Llewellyn

DOMINO BOOKS (WALES) LTD

METRIC/IMPERIAL/AMERICAN UNITS

We are all used to doubling or halving a recipe. Thus, a Victoria sandwich may be made using 4 oz each of flour, sugar and butter with 2 eggs or 6 oz each of flour, sugar and butter with 3 eggs. The proportions of the ingredients are unchanged. This must be so for all units. Use either the metric units or the imperial units given in the recipes, do not mix the two.

It is not practical to give the exact equivalents of metric and imperial units because 1 oz equals 28.35 g and 1 pint equals 568 ml. The tables on page vi indicate suitable quantities but liquids should be carefully added to obtain the correct consistency. See also the charts on page iv.

PINTS TO MILLILITRES AND LITRES
The following are approximations only

¼ pint = 150 ml   1 pint = 575 ml
½ pint = 275 ml   1 ¾ pints = 1000 ml (1 litre)
¾ pint = 425 ml   3 pints = 1 ½ litres

CONTENTS

Page

Foreword _____ v

Soups _____ 7

Savoury Dishes _____ 12

Seafood _____ 20

Meat _____ 27

Cakes _____ 36

Pastries _____ 40

Jams and Preserves _____ 44

Creams _____ 47

Units, American Equivalents _____ ii, iv, vi

Index _____ 48

© D C P and E J P, 1994. Reprinted annually 1995 - 2000
New edition 2001
Cover design and photograph Jonathan Tew
Illustration Allison Fewtrell
ISBN 1 85772 072 5

The following charts give the approximate equivalents for metric and imperial weights, and oven temperatures.

Ounces	Approx g to nearest whole number	Approx g to nearest whole 25 g
1	28	25
2	57	50
3	85	75
4	113	125
5	142	150
6	170	175
7	198	200
8	226	225
9	255	250
10	283	275
11	311	300
12	340	350
13	368	375
14	396	400
15	428	425
16	456	450

OVEN TEMPERATURE GUIDE

	Electricity °C	°F	Gas Mark
Very cool	110	225	¼
	130	250	½
Cool	140	275	1
	150	300	2
Moderate	170	325	3
	180	350	4
Moderately hot	190	375	5
	200	400	6
Hot	220	425	7
	230	450	8
Very hot	240	475	9

When using this chart for weights over 16 ounces, add the appropriate figures in the column giving the nearest whole number of grammes and then adjust to the nearest unit of 25. For example, 18 oz (16 oz + 2 oz) becomes 456 + 57 = 513 to the nearest whole number and 525 g to the nearest unit of 25.

Throughout the book, 1 teaspoon = 5 ml and 1 tablespoon = 15 ml.

FOREWORD

The word 'Celt' comes from the word 'Keltoi' used by the Greeks to describe tribes who lived north of the Alps one thousand years before the birth of Christ. Although regarded as a race, they were, in reality, many tribes with a common cultural heritage. They were skilled metal workers with a talent for decorating the things they made. Ferocious warriors, courageous in battle, the Celts loved feasting, eating, drinking, talking, singing and gambling: they often partied for several days to celebrate victories and to reward warriors for success. A boar would be roasted on a wrought iron spit and food prepared in large cauldrons. The lower classes drank mead and cider and wheaten beer called cornia prepared with honey. Aristocratic Celts drank wine neat (to the disgust of the Romans who diluted their liquor with water). Essentially, the Celts were settlers who spread across Europe, their economy based on mixed farming. The legacy from this early culture can be seen in the traditions of the six Celtic nations, Brittany, Cornwall, Ireland, Scotland, Wales and the Isle of Man.

Our ancestors knew the importance of warm soups to keep out the winter cold and summer fruits growing wild. They accepted the generosity of the sea and seashore as providers and learned to work the land. Recipes change as they are handed down and technology brings new ways of cooking. The traditional recipes in this selection have been adapted to use these new methods. I hope you will enjoy them.

S L

AMERICAN MEASURES

American measures are given by volume and weight using standard cups and spoons.

US Standard Measuring Spoons and Cups

1 tablespoon = 3 teaspoons = ½ fluid ounce = 14.2 ml
2 tablespoons = 1 fluid ounce = 28 ml
4 tablespoons = ¼ cup
5 tablespoons = ⅓ cup
8 tablespoons = ½ cup
10 tablespoons = ⅔ cup
12 tablespoons = ¾ cup
16 tablespoons = 2 cups = 8 fluid ounces = ½ US pint
32 tablespoons = 2 cups = 16 fluid ounces = 1 US pint.

Metric (Imperial)	American
1 teaspoon	1 teaspoon
1 tablespoon	1 tablespoon
1½ teaspoons	2 tablespoons
2 tablespoons	3 tablespoons
3 tablespoons	¼ (scant) cup
4 tablespoons	5 tablespoons
5 tablespoons	6 tablespoons
5½ tablespoons	7 tablespoons
6 tablespoons (scant ¼ pint)	½ cup
¼ pint	⅔ cup
scant ½ pint	1 cup
½ pint (10 fl oz)	1¼ cups
¾ pint (15 fl oz)	scant 2 cups
⅘ pint (16 fl oz)	2 cups (1 pint)
1 pint (20 fl oz)	2½ cups

Metric (Imperial)	American
flour, plain or self-raising	
15 g (½ oz)	2 tablespoons
25 g (1 oz)	1¼ cup
100/125 g (4 oz)	1 cup
sugar, caster or granulated, brown (firmly packed)	
25 g (1 oz)	2 tablespoons
100/125 g (4 oz)	½ cup
200/225 g (8 oz)	1 cup
butter, margarine, fat	
1 oz	2 tablespoons
225 g (8 oz)	1 cup
150 g (5 oz) shredded suet	1 cup

1 cup (American) contains approximately
100/125 g (4 oz) grated cheese, 50 g (2 oz) fresh breadcrumbs,
100 g (4 oz) dried breadcrumbs,
100/125 g (4 oz) pickled beetroot, button mushrooms, shelled peas, red/blackcurrants, 5 oz strawberries,
175 g (6 oz) raisins, currants, sultanas, chopped candied peel, stoned dates,
225 g (8 oz) glacé cherries, 150 g (5 oz) shelled whole walnuts,
100 g (4 oz) chopped nuts,
75 g (3 oz) desiccated coconut,
225 g (8 oz) cottage cheese,
100/125 g (4 oz) curry powder,
225 g (8 oz) minced raw meat,
⅜ pint (7½ fl oz) cream.

SOUPS

CREAMY LEEK SOUP- WALES

METRIC
25 g butter
800 g leeks
2 onions, skinned and chopped
2 celery sticks chopped
1 litre chicken stock
salt and pepper
4 tablespoons cream
fresh chives snipped - with scissors

IMPERIAL
1 oz butter
2 lb leeks
2 onions, skinned and chopped
2 celery sticks chopped
2 pints chicken stock
salt and pepper
4 tablespoons cream
fresh chives snipped - with scissors

Cook the leeks, onions and celery in the butter gently for 10 minutes until softened but not browned. Add the stock, season and bring to the boil. Cover and simmer for 30 minutes until the vegetables are cooked. Allow to cool. Purée in a blender. Serve hot. Add cream and chopped chives to individual bowls before serving.

IRISH POTATO AND PARSLEY SOUP

METRIC	IMPERIAL
2 rashers of bacon	2 rashers of bacon
25 g butter	1 oz butter
400g potatoes	1 lb potatoes
400 g onions	1 lb onions
1 litre chicken stock	2 pints chicken stock
300 ml milk	½ pint milk
salt and pepper	salt and pepper
25 g chopped parsley	1 oz chopped parsley
150 ml cream	¼ pint cream
croûtons	croûtons

Remove the rind from the bacon and fry. Peel and cut the potatoes into small cubes. Skin and slice the onions. Add the butter, potatoes and onions to the bacon in the pan. Cook for 10 minutes until the vegetables begin to soften. Add stock and milk. Season. Cover and simmer for 30 minutes until the vegetables are cooked. Purée. Return to the pan and stir in the parsley and cream. Heat but do not boil. Serve garnished with croûtons.

Croûtons: cut day old, sliced, white bread into strips then into cubes. Deep fry until golden brown. Remove with a slotted spoon and drain on kitchen paper.
[They can be stored in the freezer, taken out when needed and warmed.]

CULLEN SKINK - SCOTLAND

METRIC	IMPERIAL
1 Finnan haddock	*1 Finnan haddock*
1 litre water	*2 pints water*
1 onion skinned and chopped	*1 onion skinned and chopped*
600 ml milk	*1 pint milk*
600 g potatoes	*1 ½ lb potatoes*
Nub of butter	*Nub of butter*
salt and pepper	*salt and pepper*
chopped parsley to garnish	*chopped parsley to garnish*

Cover the haddock with boiling water. Add the onion, cover and simmer for 10 - 15 minutes until the haddock is tender. Drain the liquid and keep.

Remove the bones from the fish and flake the fish. Return the bones and the strained stock to the pan with the milk. Cover and simmer for an hour.

Peel and cook the potatoes in salted water. Drain and mash with butter. Strain the liquid from the bones and return it to the pan with the flaked fish. Add the mashed potato and stir well to give a thick creamy mixture. Season and garnish with parsley.

CHEESEY FRENCH BREAD

Cream 25 g (1 oz) butter with a crushed clove of garlic and 50 g (2 oz) grated cheese. Mix well and spread over 4 slices of French stick loaf. Grill until golden brown. (Delicious with soups.)

CRAB SOUP - BRITTANY

METRIC	IMPERIAL
1 kg small crabs	2 lb small crabs
or 300 g cooked crab meat	or 12 oz cooked crab meat
1 carrot, peeled and sliced	1 carrot, peeled and sliced
2 onions skinned and sliced	2 onions skinned and sliced
1 litre water	2 pints water
250 ml Muscadet	½ pint Muscadet
1 bouquet garni	1 bouquet garni
(thyme, bay leaf, parsley, chervil)	(thyme, bay leaf, parsley, chervil)
25 g rice	1 oz rice
salt and white peppercorns	salt and white peppercorns
cayenne pepper	cayenne pepper
8 slices lightly toasted French bread	8 slices lightly toasted French bread

Court Bouillon Put the carrot, onions, wine and bouquet garni in 1 litre (2 pints) cold water in a non-metallic saucepan and heat to boiling.

Soup Boil the rice in salted water for 17 minutes. Scrub the crabs well under running water. Add to the court bouillon, bring to the boil and cook for 5 minutes. Remove the meat from the crabs (or use cooked crab meat) and place with the rice in a blender. Liquidise. Strain the court bouillon into a saucepan and add the liquidised rice and crab meat. Season with salt, freshly ground white pepper and a pinch of cayenne pepper. Boil gently for 5 minutes. Place 2 slices of toasted bread in each of 4 bowls and ladle the soup on top.

FRENCH ONION SOUP

METRIC	IMPERIAL
50 g butter	2 oz butter
1 tablespoon cooking oil	1 tablespoon cooking oil
6 medium-sized onions, skinned and thinly sliced	6 medium-sized onions, skinned and thinly sliced
12 g flour	¼ oz flour
salt and pepper	salt and pepper
800 ml beef stock (bouillon)	1 ½ pint beef stock (bouillon)
125 ml white wine or cider	¼ pint white wine or cider
6 small slices of bread	6 small slices of bread
50 g Gruyère or Parmesan cheese, grated	2 oz Gruyère or Parmesan cheese, grated
2 tablespoons brandy (optional)	2 tablespoons brandy (optional)

Melt the butter in a thick saucepan. Add the oil and thinly sliced onions. Cook for 20 minutes until the onions are golden. Remove from the heat and stir in the flour. Season with salt and pepper. Stir in the stock and the wine or cider. Cover and simmer gently for 30 minutes until the onions are soft. Place the slices of bread in a shallow tin and bake in a moderate oven (170°C, 325°F, gas mark 3) for 30 minutes until crisp and light coloured. Pour the soup into six individual warmed soup bowls and float a round of bread on each bowl of soup. Add the brandy (optional). Serve with cheese separately.

FRENCH ONION SOUP GRATINÉE

Follow the recipe for French Onion Soup but sprinkle the grated Parmesan cheese over the bread floating on the soup. Place the bowls under the grill until the cheese melts and browns lightly. Serve immediately.

SAVOURY DISHES

WELSH FAGGOTS

METRIC	IMPERIAL
400 g pigs' liver	*1 lb pigs' liver*
2 medium sized onions, skinned	*2 medium sized onions, skinned*
75 g shredded beef suet	*3 oz shredded beef suet*
100 g breadcrumbs	*4 oz breadcrumbs*
1 teaspoon chopped sage	*1 teaspoon chopped sage*
salt and pepper	*salt and pepper*
300 ml boiling beef stock	*½ pint boiling beef stock*

Use a food processor to chop the liver and onions. Turn into a bowl. Stir in the suet, breadcrumbs and sage. Season. Roll the meat mixture into small balls and place in a well greased ovenproof dish. Pour the stock into the dish, cover and bake in a moderate oven (180ºC, 350ºF, gas mark 4) for 30 minutes. Remove the lid and cook for a further 10 minutes. Traditionally served with boiled green peas.

GARLIC MUSHROOMS WITH CREAM - BRITTANY

METRIC	IMPERIAL
300 g small white button mushrooms	*12 oz small white button mushrooms*
40 g butter	*1½ oz butter*
1 clove garlic, crushed	*1 clove garlic, crushed*
pinch of salt and freshly ground black pepper	*pinch of salt and freshly ground black pepper*
125 ml double cream	*¼ pint double cream*

Wash the mushrooms and trim the ends of the stalks. Melt the butter in the saucepan, add the garlic and mushrooms and cook for 5 minutes or until the mushrooms are tender. Garnish with parsley. Serve with lemon wedges and buttered brown bread.

FARMHOUSE CAULIFLOWER SOUFFLÉ -WALES

METRIC	IMPERIAL
200 g small cauliflower florets	*8 oz small cauliflower florets*
salt and pepper	*salt and pepper*
25 g butter	*1 oz butter*
3 tablespoons plain flour	*3 tablespoons plain flour*
200 ml milk	*⅓ pint milk*
1 tablespoon wholegrain mustard	*1 tablespoon wholegrain mustard*
100 g mature Cheddar cheese, grated	*4 oz mature Cheddar cheese, grated*
4 eggs, separated	*4 eggs, separated*

Cook the cauliflower in lightly salted water until tender. Drain. Warm the butter in a saucepan and work in the flour. Remove from the heat and stir in the milk, beating to keep the mixture smooth. Heat gently and stir until the sauce thickens. Simmer gently for 1 - 2 minutes. Add the mustard and season to taste. Turn the sauce into a blender and add the cauliflower. Purée. Add the egg yolks and cheese. Whisk the egg whites until stiff and fold into the mixture. Turn into a greased ovenproof dish. Bake in a moderate oven (180°C, 350°F, gas mark 4) for 25 - 30 minutes until browned and firm. Serve at once.

If preferred, cook the mixture in small ramekin dishes.

TEVIOTDALE PIE - SCOTLAND

METRIC	IMPERIAL
400 g lean minced beef	*1 lb lean minced beef*
1 onion, skinned and chopped	*1 onion, skinned and chopped*
300 ml beef stock	*½ pint beef stock*
1 teaspoon Worcester sauce	*1 teaspoon Worcester sauce*
salt and pepper	*salt and pepper*
200 g self raising flour	*8 oz self raising flour*
25 g cornflour	*1 oz cornflour*
75 g shredded beef suet	*3 oz shredded beef suet*
300 ml milk	*½ pint milk*

Place the meat in a saucepan and cook in its own fat over a medium heat until the meat begins to brown. Add the onion and cook for 5 minutes until the onion softens. Add the stock and Worcester sauce. Season. Simmer for 15 minutes. Mix the self raising flour, cornflour and suet in a bowl. Gradually stir in the milk to form a thick batter. Transfer the meat to a litre (2 pint) ovenproof dish. Cover with the batter mixture and bake in a moderate oven (180°C, 350°F, gas mark 4) for 30 - 35 minutes until the batter has risen and browned.

TOMATO PRAWN CUPS - WALES

Allow 25 g (1 oz) cottage cheese, 15 g (½ oz) prawns (cut up with 2 kept for decoration) for each large tomato. Cut a thin slice from the top and scoop out the pulp and seeds from each tomato. Mix the cheese and cut up prawns and fill the tomatoes. Decorate with the whole prawns and replace the tomato slices as lids. Serve with a mixed green salad.

CORNISH CAUDLE CHICKEN PIE

METRIC	IMPERIAL
25 g butter	1 oz butter
1 tablespoon olive oil	1 tablespoon olive oil
1 onion, skinned and chopped	1 onion, skinned and chopped
4 chicken drumsticks or thighs	4 chicken drumsticks or thighs
2 tablespoons chopped parsley	2 tablespoons chopped parsley
4 spring onions	4 spring onions
salt and pepper	salt and pepper
150 ml milk	¼ pint milk
200 g frozen puff pastry	8 oz frozen puff pastry
150 ml fresh soured cream	¼ pint fresh soured cream
2 eggs beaten	2 eggs beaten

Leave the pastry to thaw. Cook the onion in the butter and olive oil in a pan over a medium heat until softened but not browned. Transfer to a litre (2 pint) ovenproof dish using a slotted spoon. Skin and bone the chicken and place the meat on top of the onions. Add the parsley, spring onions, seasoning and milk to the pan and simmer for 2 - 3 minutes. Pour over the chicken. Cover and bake in a moderate oven (180°C, 350°F, gas mark 4) for 30 minutes until the chicken is cooked. Remove from the oven and leave to cool. Roll out the pastry on a floured board to a thickness of 2.5 cm (1 inch). Leave to rest while the chicken mixture is cooling. Use the pastry to cover the pie. Make a small hole in the top. Beat the soured cream and eggs together and brush the pastry lid with a little of the egg mixture. Bake in a hot oven (220°C, 425°F, gas mark 7) for 15 - 20 minutes. Reduce the temperature to 180°C, 350°F, gas mark 4. Pour the soured cream and egg mixture into the pie through the hole in the pie lid. Return to the oven and bake for 15 minutes at 180°C, 350°F, gas mark 4. Remove from the oven and leave to stand for 10 - 15 minutes before serving. Serve hot or cold.

LIKKY PIE - CORNWALL

METRIC	IMPERIAL
Shortcrust pastry	**Shortcrust pastry**
100 g plain flour	4 oz plain flour
50 g butter	2 oz butter
pinch of salt	pinch of salt
4 teaspoons cold water	4 teaspoons cold water
Filling	**Filling**
6 leeks trimmed	6 leeks trimmed
6 rashers bacon	6 rashers bacon
125 ml milk	¼ pint millk
5 tablespoons single cream	5 tablespoons single cream
2 eggs	2 eggs
salt and pepper	salt and pepper

Pastry: Sift the flour and salt together. Rub in the butter until the mixture looks like breadcrumbs. Add the water and bind into a lump.

Filling: Heat the leeks gently in salted water until softened. Drain and transfer to a greased pie dish. Cut the rind and fat off the bacon slices and place the bacon on top of the leeks. Season and pour in the milk. Cover with foil and cook for 30 minutes in a moderately hot oven (200°C, 400°F, gas mark 6). Remove the foil and allow to cool. Beat the eggs and stir the cream into them. Pour into the pie dish. Roll out the pastry and cover the pie. Brush with a little milk and bake in a moderately hot oven (190 °C, 375 °F, gas mark 5) for 30 minutes.

TYNWALD PIE - ISLE OF MAN

METRIC	IMPERIAL
6 lamb chops	6 lamb chops
25 g butter	1 oz butter
1 kg potatoes	2 lb potatoes
Gravy	**Gravy**
1 tablespoon flour	1 tablespoon flour
liquid from meat	liquid from meat

Place the chops in an ovenproof dish with 2 tablespoons water. Cover and cook in a moderate oven (180°C, 350°F, gas mark 4) for 30 minutes. Peel and boil the potatoes in salted water. Drain, keeping the water. Mash with butter. Grease a large dish and line with half of the potatoes. Place the chops on top of the potatoes using a slotted spoon. Cover with the remaining potatoes. Return to the oven for a further 10 minutes.

Gravy: Work the flour into the liquor from the lamb chops. Stir in 300 ml (½ pint) of potato water and bring to the boil. Make a hole in the potatoes in the pie dish and pour in the gravy. Serve hot with mixed vegetables including peas.

SOLLAGHAN - ISLE OF MAN

METRIC	IMPERIAL
50 g oatmeal	2 oz oatmeal
nub of butter	nub of butter
salt and pepper	salt and pepper
500 ml stock	1 pint stock

Warm the oatmeal in a pan until it is reddish in colour. Add the butter and season. Stir in the stock and stir well. (Traditionally served at Christmas.)

POTATO AND ONION PIE - IRELAND

METRIC
1 kg potatoes, peeled and sliced
200 g onions, skinned and sliced
75 g butter
salt and pepper
1 tablespoon grated cheese

IMPERIAL
2 lb potatoes, peeled and sliced
8 oz onions, skinned and sliced
3 oz butter
salt and pepper
1 tablespoon grated cheese

Fry the onions in half the butter for 3 minutes. Brush a 1.5 litre (2½ pint ovenproof dish) with a little of the butter. Put the potatoes and onions in the dish in layers, seasoning well, and finishing with a layer of potatoes. Melt the remaining butter and pour over the potatoes, making sure they are coated. Bake in a moderately hot oven, (190°C, 375°F, gas mark 5) for 1½ hours until the potatoes are cooked. Sprinkle over the cheese and brown under the grill.

SCOTTISH OATCAKES

METRIC
100 g fine oatmeal
pinch of salt
pinch of bicarbonate of soda
15 g lard
oatmeal for rolling

IMPERIAL
4 oz fine oatmeal
pinch of salt
pinch of bicarbonate of soda
½ oz lard
oatmeal for rolling

Mix the dry ingredients together. Warm the lard in 125 ml (¼ pint)water until the lard has melted. Pour enough of the liquid on to the dry ingredients to make a firm dough. Roll out on a surface sprinkled with oatmeal to a thickness of 1·25cm (½ inch) thick. Cut into 7·5 cm (3 inch) rounds. Cook on a hot griddle on one side only for 5 - 8 minutes until they curl, or place on a greased baking sheet and bake in a moderate oven (170 °C, 325 °F, gas mark 3) for 30 minutes until crisp.

JACKET POTATOES - WALES

Scrub potatoes and prick all over with a fork. Bake in a moderately hot oven 200 ℃, 400 ℉, gas mark 6 for 1 ½ hours until tender or cook on high in a microwave oven allowing 5 - 10 minutes for each potato until soft. Slit potato open and fill. (Some of the cooked potato can be removed and mashed with the filling.)

Fillings - be adventurous but taste fillings first and keep them moist with butter or dressing.

Cottage cheese and diced cucumber mixed with snipped fresh chives.

Cottage cheese and pineapple.

A selection of low fat curd cheese, natural yogurt, diced red pepper, chopped hard boiled egg seasoned and mixed together.

Lean, fried chopped bacon mixed with grated Cheddar cheese and tomato.

Lean, cooked meat (chicken, beef, pork, ham, tongue) and pickles or chutney.

Chopped turkey and cranberry sauce.

Sliced tomato, cucumber, diced carrot and mayonnaise or fromage frais.

Lettuce, coleslaw, chopped nuts and diced apple (brush the apple with lemon juice unless served at once).

Garlic sausage, chopped celery and mayonnaise.

Liver sausage blended with cream cheese, seasoned with grated onion.

Sardines or tuna or salmon with mushrooms.

Sardines with chopped hard-boiled eggs, grated cheese, butter and lemon juice.

Cooked, mashed smoked haddock mixed with snipped chives and a little lemon juice.

Smoked salmon and wedges of lemon.

Warm 25 g (1 oz) butter, 25 g (1 oz) plain flour and 300 ml (½ pint) milk together in a saucepan. Warm until sauce thickens and simmer for 1-2 minutes. Season. Stir in 50 g (2 oz) peeled prawns and 2 tablespoons of white wine. (If this is too thin, thicken with a little mashed potato.)

SEAFOOD

POACHED SALMON AND SHALLOT BUTTER - BRITTANY

METRIC	IMPERIAL
1 kg salmon steak	*2 lb salmon steak*
Court Bouillon	**Court Bouillon**
1 litre water	*2 pints water*
juice of ¼ lemon	*juice of ¼ lemon*
250 ml Muscadet	*¼ pint Muscadet*
pinch of salt	*pinch of salt*
6 black peppercorns	*6 black peppercorns*
bouquet garni	*bouquet garni*
(sprig thyme, parsley, bay leaf, stick celery)	*(sprig thyme, parsley, bay leaf, stick celery)*
Shallot Butter	**Shallot Butter**
100 g shallots, peeled and sliced	*4 oz shallots, peeled and sliced*
125 ml Muscadet wine or white wine	*¼ pint Muscadet wine or white wine*
250 ml white wine vinegar	*¼ pint white wine vinegar*
25 g butter	*1 oz butter*
salt and pepper	*salt and pepper*

Court Bouillon Put the water, lemon juice, wine, pinch of salt, peppercorns and bouquet garni in a saucepan and bring to the boil.

Poached salmon Place the fish in a shallow dish or fish kettle. Pour the court bouillon over the fish. Cover the dish and simmer very gently (the water should just move slightly) for 25 minutes until the flesh flakes easily when tested with a skewer. Carefully lift out the fish and place on a plate. Remove the skin. Serve the salmon with shallot butter, new boiled potatoes and green salad.

Shallot butter (Make after the fish has cooked because it separates and becomes oily on standing.) Place the shallots in a non metallic saucepan with the wine and vinegar. Simmer until the shallots are soft. Continue heating gently until all the liquid has evaporated. Place the pan of shallots over a saucepan of boiling water and add the butter, a small piece at a time. Beat well after each addition. Season. Use at once.

COD AND VEGETABLE PIE - CORNWALL

METRIC	IMPERIAL
1 kg cod fillets	2 lb cod fillets
50 g butter	2 oz butter
3 onions, skinned	3 onions, skinned
4 leeks, white part only	4 leeks, white part only
3 tablespoons flour	3 tablespoons flour
1 kg potatoes	2 lb potatoes
25 g breadcrumbs	1 oz breadcrumbs
salt and pepper	salt and pepper

Clean the cod and place in salted water. Bring to the boil, reduce the heat and simmer until the fish is tender. Remove the fish. Keep the liquid. Skin and bone the fish. Peel and boil the potatoes in salted water. Slice the onions and white parts of the leeks. Fry in half the butter until lightly browned. Stir in the flour. When the flour has become golden brown, slowly stir in 300 ml (½ pint) of the fish liquor to make the onion and leek sauce. Season with pepper. Continue heating with stirring until the mixture thickens. Grease a deep ovenproof dish. Break the cod into pieces and place in the dish. Cover with a layer of potatoes then with a layer of onion and leek sauce. Sprinkle with breadcrumbs and dot with butter. Bake in a hot oven (230°C, 450°F, gas mark 8) for 10 minutes. Serve with a mixed salad.

CORNISH BUTTERED LOBSTER

METRIC	IMPERIAL
2 x 1 kg cooked lobsters	*2 x 2 lb lobsters*
lemon juice	*lemon juice*
75 g butter	*3 oz butter*
4 tablespoons breadcrumbs	*4 tablespoons breadcrumbs*
3 tablespoons brandy	*3 tablespoons brandy*
3 tablespoons double cream	*3 tablespoons double cream*
salt and pepper	*salt and pepper*
pinch cayenne pepper	*pinch cayenne pepper*
cucumber slices, lemon slices, fresh dill sprigs	*cucumber slices, lemon slices, fresh dill sprigs*

Split each lobster into halves. Remove the stomach, the dark vein that runs through the body and the sponge gills. Remove the tail meat. Crack open the claws and remove the meat. Scrape the meat from the legs. Cut the meat into chunks and sprinkle with lemon juice. Remove and keep the coral. Remove and keep the soft pink flesh and liver. Scrub the shells and place in a cool oven (140°C, 275°F, gas mark 1) to warm.

Melt 25 g (1 oz) of the butter in a frying pan and add the breadcrumbs. Cook until brown. Melt the remaining butter in a saucepan, add the lobster flesh, stir and heat through. Warm the brandy in a spoon and ignite. While still flaming, pour over the lobster. Transfer the lobster to the shells and keep warm. Pound the liver and pink flesh together. Stir into the cooking juices with the cream, a pinch of salt and cayenne pepper. Spoon over the lobster. Sprinkle the fried breadcrumbs over the top. Garnish with slices of cucumber, lemon and dill sprigs.

SMOKED SALMON MOUSSE - SCOTLAND

METRIC	IMPERIAL
250 ml single cream	½ pint single cream
2 bay leaves	2 bay leaves
100 g smoked salmon	4 oz smoked salmon
1 tablespoon lemon juice	1 tablespoon lemon juice
pinch of paprika	pinch of paprika
125 ml milk	¼ pint milk
3 teaspoons gelatine	3 teaspoons gelatine

Warm the cream and bay leaves together and leave to stand for 2 hours. Remove the bay leaves. Pour the cream into a blender or food processor. Add the salmon (keep a slice for garnish), the lemon juice and paprika. Blend until smooth. Pour into a measuring jug and add milk to make the volume up to 550 ml (1 pint). Stir well. Sprinkle the gelatine over 3 tablespoons of water in a cup and leave to soak for a few minutes. Stand the cup over hot water and stir until the gelatine has dissolved. Leave to cool a little and then whisk into the salmon mixture. Pour into 6 ramekin dishes and chill for 2 hours. Serve garnished with a little smoked salmon and slices of cucumber.

SARDINE PÂTÉ - CORNWALL

Cream 50 g (2 oz) butter with 50 g (2 oz) cheese. Drain 100 g (4 oz) sardines in oil and mash. Beat into the creamed mixture with 3 tablespoons lemon juice. Season with ground black pepper. Turn into small white pots and garnish each with a bay leaf.

QUEENIES - ISLE OF MAN

METRIC	IMPERIAL
*200 g queenies, shelled	*8 oz queenies, shelled
2 small onions, skinned	2 small onions, skinned
300 ml fish stock	½ pint fish stock
salt and pepper	salt and pepper
Sauce	**Sauce**
12 g butter	½ oz butter
300 ml milk	½ pint milk
12 g flour	½ oz flour
100 g Cheddar cheese, grated	4 oz Cheddar cheese, grated
1 onion, skinned and diced	1 onion, skinned and diced

Remove any brown left on the queenies. Place the escallops in an ovenproof dish and add the onions and fish stock. Season and bake in a moderate oven (325ºC, 170ºF, gas mark 3) for 15 minutes.

Sauce Melt the butter and work in the flour. Add the milk slowly, stirring to keep the mixture free from lumps. Add the diced onion and grated cheese. Heat gently. Pour the sauce over the scallops and serve with green salad.

* These are small shellfish, a variety of escallop caught by Manxmen off the shores of the island. They have a delicious, delicate flavour which is spoiled if they are over-cooked.

MANX KIPPERS

Dot the kippers with butter and grill on both sides for 3 - 4 minutes. Serve with buttered brown bread.

SEWIN WITH HERB SAUCE - WALES

METRIC	IMPERIAL
1 kg sewin (sea trout)	*2 lb sewin (sea trout)*
3 tablespoons lemon juice	*3 tablespoons lemon juice*
50 g butter	*2 oz butter*
salt and pepper	*salt and pepper*
1 bunch watercress, trimmed	*1 bunch watercress, trimmed*
50 g spinach leaves	*2 oz spinach leaves*
3 tablespoons fresh parsley	*3 tablespoons fresh parsley*
2 tablespoons fresh chervil	*2 tablespoons fresh chervil*
1 teaspoon chopped fresh dill	*1 teaspoon chopped fresh dill*
125 ml mayonnaise	*¼ pint mayonnaise*
fresh herbs or whole, unpeeled cooked prawns	*fresh herbs or whole, unpeeled cooked prawns*
for garnish	*for garnish*

Clean the fish and place in a piece of foil. Add 2 tablespoons lemon juice and dot with 25 g (1 oz) of butter. Season. Close the foil and place on a baking sheet. Cook in a moderate oven (1805°C, 350°F, gas mark 4) for 10 minutes per 400 g (per pound) until the fish is cooked. Remove the fish from the foil, keeping the liquor. Remove the skin from the fish and leave the fish on a dish to cool. Put the fish liquor and remaining butter in a pan and heat gently. Chop the watercress, spinach, parsley, chervil and dill and add to the pan. Cook for 2 - 3 minutes. Put into a food processor and blend until smooth. Transfer to a bowl and add remaining lemon juice. Season. Leave until cold. Fold in the mayonnaise. Refrigerate until required. To serve, pour the sauce over the fish and garnish with fresh herbs and prawns.

FRESH TUNA CASSEROLE - BRITTANY

METRIC	IMPERIAL
1 kg tuna steak	*2 lb tuna steak*
4 slices bacon	*4 slices bacon*
75 g butter	*3 oz butter*
125 g baby onions, peeled	*5 oz baby onions, peeled*
1 glass Muscadet or dry white wine	*1 glass Muscadet or dry white wine*
250 ml vegetable broth	*¼ pint vegetable broth*
1 bouquet garni (bay leaf, parsley, thyme)	*1 bouquet garni (bay leaf, parsley, thyme)*
1 lettuce heart	*1 lettuce heart*
3 medium sized carrots, peeled	*3 medium sized carrots, peeled*
1 small turnip	*1 small turnip*
400 g frozen peas	*1 lb frozen peas*
salt and pepper	*salt and pepper*

Remove the skin and bones from the fish. Wrap in the bacon slices and tie. Place the onions in a deep pan and sauté in the butter until lightly browned. Add the tuna and cook for a few minutes on each side. Add the wine and vegetable broth and the bouquet garni. Bring to the boil. Cover and simmer for 45 minutes. Rinse and dry the lettuce and cut up. Place around the tuna. Cut the carrots into matchstick pieces. Peel and cut up the turnip. Add the vegetables to the casserole. Cover and simmer gently for 20 minutes. Add the peas and simmer until the vegetables are cooked. Place the tuna on a hot plate and remove the bacon. Transfer the fish to a warm serving dish. Arrange the vegetables around the fish. Remove the bouquet garni from the liquor and pour the liquor over the fish.

MEAT

ANGUS BEEF IN WHISKY SAUCE - SCOTLAND

METRIC	IMPERIAL
1 kg sirloin steak	*2 lb sirloin steak*
15 g butter	*½ oz butter*
1 onion, skinned and chopped	*1 onion, skinned and chopped*
3 tablespoons whisky liqueur, e g Drambuie	*3 tablespoons whisky liqueur, e g Drambuie*
3 tablespoons double cream	*3 tablespoons double cream*
salt and pepper	*salt and pepper*

Melt the butter in a pan. Cut the steak into strips and add to the pan with the onion. Cook to taste. Stir in the liqueur and cream. Heat gently but do not boil. Serve with mixed vegetables and new potatoes.

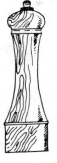

BEEF POCKETS - SCOTLAND

METRIC
4 thick beef steaks
15 g butter
150 g mushrooms
1 garlic clove, skinned and crushed
1 large onion, skinned and chopped
1 tablespoon chopped fresh parsley
1 tablespoon ginger wine
1 tablespoon breadcrumbs
1 tablespoon double cream
salt and pepper

IMPERIAL
4 thick beef steaks
½ oz butter
6 oz mushrooms
1 garlic clove, skinned and crushed
1 large onion, skinned and chopped
1 tablespoon chopped fresh parsley
1 tablespoon ginger wine
1 tablespoon breadcrumbs
1 tablespoon double cream
salt and pepper

Make a horizontal cut in each steak - do not cut right through the meat. Melt the butter in a pan and cook the mushrooms, garlic and onion for 5 minutes. Season. Remove from the heat and add the parsley, ginger wine, breadcrumbs and cream. Mix well and spoon into the steak pockets. Grill the steaks for 5 - 10 minutes to taste. Serve with new potatoes and mixed vegetables or a mixed salad.

BACON CHOPS IN CIDER - CORNWALL

METRIC
4 bacon chops each weighing 150 g
1 tablespoon prepared English mustard
25 g demerara sugar
15 g butter
1 tablespoon plain flour
salt and pepper, chopped fresh parsley

IMPERIAL
4 bacon chops each weighing 6 oz
1 tablespoon prepared English mustard
1 oz demerara sugar
½ oz butter
1 tablespoon plain flour
salt and pepper, chopped fresh parsley

Place the chops in an ovenproof dish. Mix the mustard and sugar with 2 tablespoons cider to make a smooth paste. Spread over the chops and leave to stand for 30 minutes. Bake the chops in a moderately hot oven (200°C, 400°F, gas mark 6) for 15 minutes. Warm the butter in a saucepan and work in the flour. Add the rest of the cider, stirring to keep the sauce free from lumps. Heat until the sauce boils and thickens. Simmer for 1 - 2 minutes. Season. Pour the sauce over the chops. Cover and bake for a further 15 minutes until the chops are cooked. Garnish with parsley.

WINTER CASSEROLE - BRITTANY

METRIC	IMPERIAL
1 kg beef	*2 lb beef*
400 g unsmoked bacon	*1 lb unsmoked bacon*
1 onion, peeled and studded with a clove	*1 onion, peeled and studded with a clove*
1 bouquet garni (thyme, bay leaf, parsley)	*1 bouquet garni (thyme, bay leaf, parsley)*
2 leeks, chopped	*2 leeks, chopped*
2 carrots, peeled and sliced	*2 carrots, peeled and sliced*
1 small turnip, peeled and chopped	*1 small turnip, peeled and chopped*
1 cabbage heart, quartered	*1 cabbage heart, quartered*
1 smoked boiling sausage	*1 smoked boiling sausage*

Place the beef, bacon, onion and bouquet garni in a large saucepan. Cover with cold water and bring to the boil. Cover and simmer gently for 1½ hours, removing any scum from the surface. Blanch the cabbage heart in boiling water before cutting it up. Add the vegetables and bring back to the boil. Simmer for 20 minutes. Prick the skin of the sausage and add to the casserole. Simmer for a further 30 minutes.

HONEYED WELSH LAMB

METRIC	IMPERIAL
1.5 kg shoulder of Welsh lamb, boned	*3 lb shoulder of Welsh lamb, boned*
salt and pepper	*salt and pepper*
1 teaspoon ground ginger	*1 teaspoon ground ginger*
2 tablespoons chopped chives	*2 tablespoons chopped chives*
4 tablespoons chopped parsley	*4 tablespons chopped parsley*
1 teaspoon fresh lemon thyme	*1 teaspoon fresh lemon thyme*
1 teaspoon chopped rosemary	*1 teaspoon chopped rosemary*
3 - 4 tablespoons honey	*3 - 4 tablespoons honey*
300 ml cider	*½ pint cider*

Lay the lamb flat. Season lightly with salt and pepper. Mix the herbs and ginger together and sprinkle over the meat. Roll up the meat and tie. Place in a roasting tin. Pour over the honey and cider. Roast in a hot oven (220°C, 425°F, gas mark 7) for 30 minutes and then reduce the heat to 200°C, 400°F, gas mark 6 until the meat is cooked. Allow 20 minutes per 400 g (per pound). Baste during the cooking. If the meat starts to burn, cover with foil. Remove the lamb. Remove excess fat and use honey and cider liquor as gravy. Serve with creamed or boiled new potatoes and peas.

LAMB IN RED WINE - WALES

Omit the honey and cider from the above recipe. Remove the cooked lamb from the roasting tin. Skim excess fat from the liquor in the tin and stir in 300 ml (½ pint) red wine. Boil for a few minutes until the gravy thickens. Pour over the meat when serving.

ROAST LEG OF LAMB WITH WHITE BEANS - BRITTANY

METRIC	IMPERIAL
2 kg leg of lamb	4 lb leg of lamb
1 bouquet garni (parsley,	1 bouquet garni (parsley
bay leaf, summer savory or thyme)	bay leaf, summer savory or thyme)
400 g dried white kidney beans	1 lb dried white kidney beans
2 medium size tomatoes	2 medium size tomatoes
2 cloves garlic, peeled	2 cloves garlic, peeled
25 g butter	1 oz butter
3 medium size onions, skinned and chopped	3 medium size onions, skinned and chopped
2 shallots, skinned and chopped	2 shallots, skinned and chopped
salt and pepper	salt and pepper
Gravy	Gravy
1 tablespoon flour	1 tablespoon flour

Soak the kidney beans in cold water overnight. Next day, place the beans in a large saucepan and cover with unsalted cold water. Add the bouquet garni and whole tomatoes. Boil for 45 minutes. Add a pinch of salt and continue to boil until the beans are tender. When the beans are nearly cooked, heat the butter in a saucepan and add the onions and shallots. Remove the tomatoes from the beans and skin. Cut up the flesh of the tomatoes and add to the onions. Heat gently until the onions are soft. Add the drained beans keeping back 250 ml ($\frac{1}{4}$ pint) of the liquid. Season with pepper. Transfer to a serving dish and keep hot.

Meat: Make slits between the bone and flesh at the knuckle end of the leg of lamb and push in the garlic cloves. Grease a roasting pan with butter and dot with small pieces of butter. Season. Roast in a moderately hot oven (190°C, 375°F, gas mark 5) for 1 hour until the meat is cooked. To crisp the fat, prick with a fork ten minutes before cooking is complete. Remove the cooked meat from the pan and keep warm.

Gravy: Remove excess fat from the roasting tin and work the flour into the meat juices left. Add water from the beans. Bring to the boil. Stir and heat until thickened. Serve the meat with the beans and pour over the gravy.

DUCK À L'ORANGE - BRITTANY

METRIC
1 x 1.5 kg duckling
salt and pepper
watercress for garnish
Sauce
2 oranges
250 ml water
1 tablespoon cognac
1 teaspoon sugar
1 tablespoon flour
250 ml duck stock, water or potato/vegetable water
125 ml dry white wine
salt and freshly ground black pepper
juice of 1 orange

IMPERIAL
1 x 3 lb duckling
salt and pepper
watercress for garnish
Sauce
2 oranges
⅟ pint water
1 tablespoon cognac
1 teaspoon sugar
1 tablespoon flour
⅟ pint duck stock, water or potato/vegetable water
⅟ pint dry white wine
salt and freshly ground black pepper
juice of 1 orange

Wipe the duck inside and out and sprinkle with salt and pepper. Place in a roasting tin and cover with foil. Cook in a moderately hot oven (190ºC, 375ºF, gas mark 5) allowing 20 minutes per 400 gm (per lb). Baste frequently. 10 minutes before cooking is complete, remove the foil and prick the duck all all over with a fork. Raise the temperature of the oven to 220ºC, 425ºF, gas mark 7 for 10 minutes to crisp the skin.

Sauce: Peel the oranges very thinly using a potato peeler. Cut the rind into very fine shreds and simmer in hot water for 3 minutes. Drain and keep for garnish. Remove the pith from the oranges and cut them into sections. Sprinkle with brandy and leave to stand. Transfer the duck to an ovenproof dish and return to the oven to keep warm. (Oven should be off.) Pour away all but about 2 tablespoons of the fat and liquor in the roasting tin. Add the sugar and warm to caramelize. Work in the flour. Stir in the stock or potato/vegetable water and cook gently until the sauce thickens. Add the wine and orange juice. Season to taste. Cool gently for 5 minutes. Add a few of the shreds of orange peel.

Serve duck garnished with orange sections and watercress. Pour over the sauce. Serve with boiled new potatoes and peas.

[**Stock** can be made by boiling duck's feet, neck etc with a carrot, 1 teaspoon black pepper corns and bouquet garni in water for several hours or for 45 minutes in a pressure cooker. Strain before using.]

CHICKEN IN CIDER WITH MUSHROOMS - CORNWALL

METRIC
1 medium size chicken
250 ml dry cider
1 onion, skinned and chopped
salt and ground black pepper
500 ml milk (approx)
50 g butter
50 g flour
200 g button mushrooms, sliced
chopped parsley and croûtons
salt and pepper

IMPERIAL
1 medium size chicken
¼ pint dry cider
1 onion, skinned and chopped
salt and ground black pepper
1 pint milk (approx)
2 oz butter
2 oz flour
8 oz button mushrooms, sliced
chopped parsley and croûtons
salt and pepper

Clean the chicken and put it in a casserole dish. Add the cider and chopped onion. Season. Cover with a lid or foil and cook in a moderate oven (180°C, 350°F, gas mark 4). Allow 20 minutes per 500 g (per lb) and 20 minutes over. When cooked, lift the chicken out of the dish. Strain the liquid in the casserole dish and make it up to 750 ml (1¼ pints) with milk. Remove the meat from the chicken and cut into pieces. Melt the butter in a deep pan and sauté the mushrooms. Sprinkle over the flour and stir until well blended. Stir in the chicken stock and milk. Cook for 2 minutes on a low heat. Season. Stir in the chicken and warm through. Turn into a warm serving dish. Sprinkle with chopped parsley and serve garnished with fried bread croûtons and a green salad or mixed vegetables.

BEEF IN STOUT - WALES

METRIC	IMPERIAL
1 kg stewing steak	*2 lb stewing steak*
25 g butter	*1 oz butter*
1 tablespoon vegetable oil	*1 tablespoon vegetable oil*
4 medium size onions, skinned and sliced	*4 medium size onions, skinned and sliced*
100 g button mushrooms	*4 oz button mushrooms*
salt and pepper	*salt and pepper*
2 tablespoons flour	*2 tablespoons flour*
300 ml stout	*½ pint stout*
1 bay leaf	*1 bay leaf*
1 teaspoon soft dark brown sugar	*1 teaspoon soft dark brown sugar*

Cut the steak into 5 cm (2 inch) cubes. Cook the meat in the butter and oil in a pan for 10 minutes until it is browned all over. Remove the meat using a slotted spoon. Halve the mushrooms and add to the pan with the onions. Fry until softened. Season. Remove the pan from the heat. Sprinkle over the flour so that it absorbs the fat. Return the meat to the pan. Stir in the stout. Add bay leaf and brown sugar. Mix well. Turn into an ovenproof dish, cover and cook in a moderate oven (180°C, 350°F, gas mark 4) for 2½ hours until the meat is tender.

CHICKEN IN CREAM - CORNWALL

METRIC	IMPERIAL
25 g butter	*1 oz butter*
1 tablespoon vegetable oil	*1 tablespoon vegetable oil*
4 chicken pieces	*4 chicken pieces*
salt and pepper	*salt and pepper*
125 ml double cream	*½ pint double cream*

Heat the butter and oil in a deep pan. Fry the chicken pieces until lightly browned all over. Transfer to an ovenproof casserole dish. Season. Pour over the cream and cook in a moderately hot oven (200°C, 400°F, gas mark 6) for 45 minutes - 1 hour until the chicken is cooked. Serve garnished with parsley.

SPICED BEEF - IRELAND

METRIC	IMPERIAL
2 kg salted rolled silverside	4 lb salted rolled silverside
1 onion, skinned and sliced	1 onion, skinned and sliced
4 carrots, peeled and sliced	4 carrots, peeled and sliced
1 small turnip, peeled and cut up	1 small turnip, peeled and cut up
8 cloves	8 cloves
100 g brown sugar	4 oz brown sugar
¼ teaspoon mustard powder	¼ teaspoon mustard powder
1 teaspoon ground cinnamon	1 teaspoon ground cinnamon
juice of 1 lemon	juice of 1 lemon

Soak the meat in water overnight. Rinse and place in a large saucepan or casserole dish. Add the vegetables. Cover with water and bring to the boil. Skim and season. Cover the saucepan or dish and simmer slowly for 3 hours. Leave to cool in the liquid. Remove the meat and drain well. Transfer to a roasting tin and stick the cloves in the fat of the meat. Mix the sugar, mustard, cinnamon and lemon juice together and spread over the meat. Bake in a moderate oven (180°C, 350°F, gas mark 4) for 45 minutes basting occasionally. Remove the cloves and serve hot or cold.
The meat may be pressed after cooking. Place the beef in a tight fitting dish and spoon a little of the liquor from the roasting tin over it. Put a board or plate with a heavy weight on top of the meat and leave in a cool place overnight.

CAKES

RASPBERRY AND WALNUT SHORTBREAD - SCOTLAND

METRIC	IMPERIAL
100 g walnut, chopped	4 oz walnuts, chopped
100 g butter	4 oz butter
75 g caster sugar	3 oz caster sugar
100 g plain flour	4 oz plain flour
50 g rice flour	2 oz rice flour
400 g fresh raspberries	1 lb fresh raspberries
50 g icing sugar	2 oz icing sugar
2 tablespoons kirsch (optional)	2 tablespoons kirsch (optional)
300 ml whipping cream	½ pint whipping cream

Finely grind the chopped walnuts in a food processor or blender. Cream the butter and sugar together until the mixutre is pale cream in colour and fluffy. Beat in the ground walnuts. Work in the flours. Draw the mixture together and knead lightly. Divide the mixture into three equal parts. Sprinkle a little flour on the palm of your hand and press each portion into a circle about 20 cm (8 in) in diameter. Place on non-stick baking parchment on a baking tray. Cut one of the shortbread circles into 8 triangles. Prick the shortbread all over using a fork so that moisture is released while baking and the shortbread is crisp. Bake in a moderately hot oven (190°C, 375°F, gas mark 5) for 15 - 20 minutes until the shortbread is browned evenly all over. Put two-thirds of the raspberries, icing sugar and kirsch (if used) in a bowl and mash the fruit with a fork. Leave to stand for a few minutes. Just before serving, whip the cream and fold into the fruit mixture. Use half the mixture to sandwich the two shortbread circles together and then spread the rest of the fruit mixture over the top circle. Put the shortbread triangles on top, placing them at an angle so that they form a peak in the centre. Place the remaining raspberries beween the triangles. Serve at once.

STRAWBERRY AND WALNUT SHORTBREAD - SCOTLAND

Replace the raspberries by strawberries in the recipe for Raspberry and Walnut Shortbread.

CIDER CAKE - CORNWALL

METRIC	IMPERIAL
125 ml dry cider	¼ pint dry cider
100 g sultanas	4 oz sultanas
100 g butter	4 oz butter
100 g light brown sugar	4 oz light brown sugar
2 eggs, beaten	2 eggs, beaten
200 g plain flour	8 oz plain flour
1 teaspoon bicarbonate of soda	1 teaspoon bicarbonate of soda

Mix the cider and sultanas in a large bowl. Cover with a cloth and leave to stand overnight. Grease an 18 cm (7 inch) square cake tin. Cream the butter and sugar together until the mixture is creamy in colour and fluffy. Gradually beat in the eggs, one at a time. Add half the flour and bicarbonate of soda. Beat well. Add the sultanas and cider and mix well. Fold in the rest of the flour. Pour the cake mixture into the tin and bake in a moderate oven (180°C, 350°F, gas mark 4) for 1 hour until the cake remains firm to the touch. Leave to cool in the tin for 30 minutes and then turn out on to a wire tray. Leave to cool then cut into squares.

GINGERBREAD - SCOTLAND

METRIC	IMPERIAL
200 g plain flour	8 oz plain flour
pinch of salt	pinch of salt
2 teaspoons baking powder	2 teaspoons baking powder
1 teaspoon ground ginger	1 teaspoon ground ginger
½ teaspoon ground mixed spice	½ teaspoon ground mixed spice
50 g butter	2 oz butter
2 tablespoons treacle (molasses)	2 tablespoons treacle (molasses)
75 g dark brown sugar	3 oz dark brown sugar
2 eggs, beaten	2 eggs, beaten
150 ml milk	¼ pint milk
1 teaspoon bicarbonate of soda	1 teaspoon bicarbonate of soda
lemon glacé icing.	lemon glacé icing.

Sift the flour, baking powder, ginger, spice and salt together. Cream the butter with the treacle and sugar. Dissolve the bicarbonate of soda in the milk. Stir the flour mixture, eggs and milk into the treacle mixture. Beat until the surface of the mixture is covered with bubbles. Line a greased 20 cm (8 inch) square cake tin with greased greaseproof paper. Pour in the cake mixture and bake in a moderate oven (180ºC, 350ºF, gas mark 4) for 30 - 35 minutes. When cool, store in an airtight tin for 1 - 2 days before coating with lemon glacé icing.

LEMON GLACÉ ICING

Sift 150 g (6 oz) icing sugar into a bowl and slowly add 1 tablespoon lemon juice. Mix to a smooth paste that coats the back of a spoon. Pour over the top of the cake, smoothing with the flat of a knife that has been dipped in hot water.

HONEY AND CHOCOLATE CAKE - WALES

METRIC
150 g butter
150 g brown sugar
125 g clear honey
2 eggs
1 tablespoon rum (optional)
¼ teaspoon vanilla essence
2 tablespoons unsweetened cocoa powder
175 g self-raising flour
pinch of salt
125 ml sweet sherry
250 ml double cream
2 teaspoons icing sugar, sifted

IMPERIAL
6 oz butter
6 oz brown sugar
5 oz clear honey
2 eggs
1 tablespoon rum (optional)
¼ teaspoon vanilla essence
2 tablespoons unsweetened cocoa powder
7 oz self raising flour
pinch of salt
¼ pint sweet sherry
¼ pint double cream
2 teaspoons icing sugar, sifted

Line two greased 18 cm (7 inch) round cake tins with greased greaseproof paper. Cream the butter and brown sugar together. Add the honey and beat until light and fluffy. Beat in the eggs, one at a time, then stir in the rum and vanilla essence. Sift the cocoa, flour and salt together. Fold the flour mixture and sherry alternately into the honey mixture. Divide equally between the cake tins. Bake in a moderate oven (1805°C, 350°F, gas mark 4) for 25 minutes until firm to the touch. Turn onto a wire rack to cool. Sandwich together with the whipped cream. Dust with icing sugar.

PASTRIES

JAM AND CREAM SPLITS - CORNWALL

METRIC	IMPERIAL
200 g self raising flour	*8 oz self raising flour*
75 g butter	*3 oz butter*
50 g caster sugar	*2 oz caster sugar*
3 teaspoons milk	*3 teaspoons milk*
pinch of salt	*pinch of salt*
clotted cream	*clotted cream*
strawberry jam	*strawberry jam*

Sift the flour and salt together. Rub in the butter until the mixture looks like breadcrumbs. Stir in the sugar. Add enough milk to make a stiff dough. Turn on to a floured board and knead lightly. Form into rolls and brush with milk. Bake on a greased baking sheet in a moderately hot oven (200°C, 400°F, gas mark 4) for 10 - 15 minutes until well risen. Allow to cool. To serve, split and sandwich with clotted cream and strawberry jam.

CHOCOLATE CREAM FANCIES - CORNWALL

METRIC	IMPERIAL
75 g self raising flour	*3 oz self raising flour*
pinch of salt	*pinch of salt*
3 teaspoons cocoa powder	*3 teaspoons cocoa powder*
100 g butter	*4 oz butter*
100 g caster sugar	*4 oz caster sugar*
2 eggs, beaten	*2 eggs, beaten*

Sieve the flour and salt together. Cream the fat and sugar until creamy and fluffy. Beat in the eggs, one at a time. Fold in the flour. Spoon into 18 greased patty tins and bake in a moderately hot oven (200°C, 400°F, gas mark 6) for 10 minutes. Remove the cakes from the tins and cool on a wire tray.

Decorate with whipped cream, chocolate drops and crushed chocolate flake.

ALMOND AND CALVADOS COOKIES - BRITTANY

METRIC	IMPERIAL
250 g self raising flour	*10 oz self raising flour*
25 g butter	*1 oz butter*
75 g caster sugar	*3 oz caster sugar*
2 egg yolks	*2 egg yolks*
75 g ground almonds	*3 oz ground almonds*
3 tablespoons double cream	*3 tablespoons double cream*
3 tablespoons calvados or apple juice	*3 tablespoons calvados or apple juice*

Sift the flour into a bowl. Warm the butter to soften it and cut into pieces. Add all the ingredients to the bowl and work into the flour using a wooden spoon. Knead lightly and form into a ball. Wrap in foil and chill for 30 minutes. Roll out on a floured board of 0.5 cm (¼ inch) and cut into 5 cm (2 inch) rounds. Place on a greased baking tray. Brush with cold milk and bake in a hot oven (220°C, 425°F, gas mark 7) for 10 - 15 minutes until golden brown.

APRICOT AND ALMOND TART - BRITTANY

METRIC
Pastry
150 g plain flour
100 g butter
1 egg yolk
1 tablespoon caster sugar
2 teaspoons cold water
Crème pâtissière
3 egg yolks
75 g caster sugar
½ teaspoon vanilla essence
25 g flour
300 ml milk
Filling
600 g apricots
juice of ½ lemon
6 tablespoons water
50 g caster sugar
Glaze
½ teaspoon arrowroot
1 tablespoon brandy
15 g toasted flaked almonds

IMPERIAL
Pastry
6 oz plain flour
4 oz butter
1 egg yolk
1 tablespoon caster sugar
2 teaspoons cold water
Crème pâtissière
3 egg yolks
3 oz caster sugar
½ teaspoon vanilla essence
1 oz flour
½ pint milk
Filling
1 ½ lb apricots
juice of ½ lemon
6 tablespoons water
2 oz caster sugar
Glaze
½ teaspoon arrowroot
1 tablespoon brandy
½ oz toasted flaked almonds

Pastry: Rub the butter into the flour until the mixture looks like breadcrumbs. Mix the egg yolk, caster sugar and water and stir into the flour mixture. Bind together. Roll out on a floured board and use to line a 22.5 cm (9 inch) flan tin. Chill for 30 minutes. Line the flan case with greaseproof paper and baking beans. Bake blind in a hot oven (220°C,

425°F, gas mark 7) for 10 minutes. Remove the beans and greaseproof paper and cook for a further 5 minutes. Cool then carefully lift on to a serving dish.

Crème pâtissière: Place egg yolks, sugar, vanilla essence and flour with a little milk in a bowl and whisk to a smooth mixture using a wire whisk. Boil the rest of the milk and pour into the mixture, whisking to keep the mixture smooth. Rinse the milk saucepan then return the mixture to the saucepan and stir over a low heat until the custard has thickened. Remove from the heat and when cool spread over the flan case.

Filling: Wash and halve the apricots, removing the stones. Put the lemon juice and water in a shallow pan. Add the apricots, cut side down and sprinkle with sugar. Cover with a tight-fitting lid. Bring to the boil and simmer gently for 5 minutes until the fruit is just soft. Lift out with a slotted spoon and arrange on top of the crème pâtissière.

Glaze: Mix the arrowroot with brandy and then add the juices from the pan. Return to the pan and heat gently until the glaze thickens. If it becomes too thick, add a little water. Add almonds to glaze and spoon over the apricots. Serve with whipped cream.

PEACH FLAN - WALES

Replace the apricots in the recipe for apricot and almond tart by skinned peaches. If tinned peaches are used, they do not need to be cooked. Glaze and serve with whipped cream.

STRAWBERRY AND CREAM FLAN - CORNWALL

Make the flan case as in the recipe for apricot and almond tart. Wash and hull 400 g (1 lb) strawberries. Cut in half, keeping some for the top. Fill the flan with strawberry halves and top with whipped cream. Decorate with whole strawberries.

JAMS AND PRESERVES

BLACKBERRY AND APPLE JAM - WALES

METRIC
600 g cooking apples, peeled, cored and sliced
250 ml water
2 kg blackberries, washed
3 kg sugar

IMPERIAL
1 ⅓ lb cooking apples, peeled, cored and sliced
⅓ pint water
4 lb blackberries, washed
6 lb sugar

Simmer the apples in half the water until they are soft. Mash with a spoon. Simmer the blackberries in half the water until they are soft. Add the blackberries and sugar to the apples, bring to the boil and boil rapidly, stirring until setting point is reached. Pot in sterilised jars and cover.
Setting point: Remove the pan from the heat. Put a little of the jam on a cold saucer and allow it to cool. Push the finger across the top of the jam. When setting point has been reached, the surface will wrinkle. (Setting point is reached at 105°C, 221°F.)

APRICOT JAM - CORNWALL

METRIC
400 g dried apricots
1500 ml water
juice of 1 lemon
1200 g sugar

IMPERIAL
1 lb dried apricots
3 pints water
juice of 1 lemon
3 lb sugar

Soak the apricots in water for 24 hours. Transfer the fruit and water to a pan and simmer for 30 minutes, stirring from time to time. Add the sugar and lemon juice. Stir over a low heat until the sugar has dissolved. Boil rapidly until setting point is reached. (See recipe for blackberry and apple jam.) Skim and pot in warm, sterilised jars. Cover.

PEACH JAM - CORNWALL

Replace the apricots in the recipe for apricot jam by peaches and use 1000 ml (2 pints) water only.

PEARS AND CHERRIES IN WHITE PORT - SCOTLAND

METRIC	IMPERIAL
600 ml white port or white wine	1 pint white port or white wine
1 kg sugar	2 lb sugar
600 ml water	1 pint water
2.5 cm cinnamon stick	1 inch cinnamon stick
450 g Morello cherries	1 lb Morello cherries
2 kg pears, peeled, cored and halved	4 lb pears, peeled, cored and halved

Add the sugar, water and cinnamon stick to the port or wine and bring to the boil. Add the cherries and simmer until the syrup is thick and the cherries are slightly softened. Add the pears and simmer for 2 minutes but do not allow the pears to become soft. Pour into warm, sterilised jars, filling the jars completely, and seal.

APPLE CHUTNEY - CORNWALL

METRIC	IMPERIAL
1 ¼ kg apples, peeled, cored and chopped	3 lb apples, peeled, cored and chopped
400 g sultanas	1 lb sultanas
150 g preserved ginger, chopped	6 oz preserved ginger, chopped
900 ml vinegar	1 ½ pints vinegar
800 g sugar	2 lb sugar
12 g salt	½ oz salt
½ teaspoon allspice	½ teaspoon allspice

Mix the vinegar, sugar, salt and spice together and bring to the boil. Add the apples and simmer for 10 minutes. Add the ginger and sultanas. Do not cover and heat gently until the mixture thickens. Pot in warm, sterilised jars and seal. Leave for several weeks for the flavour to develop.

MIXED PICKLES - WALES

Soak a selection of vegetables such as cauliflower florets, cucumber (peeled and diced), skinned shallots and sliced French beans in salt water overnight. Remove from the brine and rinse. Dry well with a cloth or kitchen paper. Pack in jars and cover with cold spiced vinegar.
Spiced vinegar: Use an enamel-lined, aluminium or stainless steel saucepan. Mix 1 litre (2 pints) vinegar with 2 tablespoons blades of mace, 1 tablespoon whole allspice, 1 tablespoon cloves, 15 cm (6 inch) cinnamon stick and 6 peppercorns. Bring to the boil and then pour into a bowl, cover and leave to cool for 2 hours. Strain before using. A better flavour is obtained if the spices are left to stand in unheated vinegar for 2 months.
[25 g (1 oz) pickling spice can be used instead of the different spices.]

CREAMS

CRÈMES AU CHOCOLAT - BRITANNY

METRIC	IMPERIAL
2 eggs, separated	2 eggs, separated
100 g plain chocolate	4 oz plain chocolate
75 g unsalted butter	3 oz unsalted butter
75 g caster sugar	3 oz caster sugar
thinly pared orange rind, grated	thinly pared orange rind, grated
125 ml double cream	¼ pint double cream

Break the chocolate into small pieces and melt in a bowl standing over hot water. Remove the basin from the heat and stir in the butter and sugar. Add the egg yolks, one at a time, beating well after each addition. Add the grated orange rind, keeping some for decoration. Whisk the egg whites until they are stiff and fold into the mixture. Spoon into ramekin dishes and chill. To serve, decorate with whipped cream and flakes of orange rind.

ORANGE CREAMS - CORNWALL

Grate the rind of 1 orange into a bowl. Cut 4 thin slices from another orange for decoration. Squeeze the juice from both oranges. Mix the grated orange rind, juice and 25 g (1 oz) caster sugar into 250 ml (¼ pint) double cream with 2 teaspoons lemon juice. Crumble a sponge finger into the bottom of each of 4 glasses and stand 2 sponge fingers against the sides of each glass. Pour over the orange cream. Decorate with orange slices and chill.

INDEX

[**Key:** B - Brittany, C - Cornwall, I - Ireland, M - Isle of Man, S- Scotland, W - Wales]

Angus beef in whisky sauce [S], 27
Apple chutney [C], 46
Apricot jam [C], 44
Almond and calvados cookies [B], 41
Apricot and almond tart [B], 42
Bacon chops in cider [C], 28
Beef in stout [W], 34
Beef pockets [S], 28
Blackberry and apple jam [W], 44
Cakes, 36
Cheesey French bread, 9
Chocolate cream fancies [C], 40
Chicken in cider with
    mushrooms [C], 33
Chicken in cream [C], 34
Cider cake [C], 37
Cod and vegetable pie [C], 21
Cornish buttered lobster, 22
Cornish caudle chicken pie, 15
Crab soup [B], 10
Creams, 47
Crèmes au chocolat [B], 47
Creamy leek soup [W], 7
Cullen skink [S], 9
Duck à l'orange [B], 32
Farmhouse cauliflower

soufflé [W], 13
French onion soup, 11
French onion soup gratinée, 11
Fresh tuna casserole [B], 26
Garlic mushrooms
    with cream [B], 12
Gingerbread [S], 38
Honey and chocolate
    cake [W], 39
Honeyed Welsh lamb, 30
Irish potato and parsley soup, 8
Jacket potatoes [W], 19
Jam and cream splits [C], 40
Jams, 44
Lamb in red wine [W], 30
Lemon glacé icing, 38
Likky pie [C], 16
Manx kippers, 24
Meat, 27
Mixed pickles [W], 46
Orange creams [C], 47
Peach flan [W], 43
Pastries, 40
Peach jam [C], 45
Pears and cherries
    in white port [S], 45

Poached salmon and
    shallot butter [B], 20
Potato and onion pie [I], 18
Preserves, 44
Queenies [M], 24
Raspberry and walnut
    shortbread [S], 36
Roast leg of lamb with
    white beans [B], 31
Savoury dishes, 12
Sardine pâté [C], 23
Seafood, 20
Scottish oatcakes, 18
Sewin with herb sauce [W], 25
Smoked salmon mousse [S], 23
Sollaghan [M], 17
Soups, 7
Spiced beef [I], 35
Strawberry and cream flan [C], 43
Strawberry and
    walnut shortbread [S], 37
Teviotdale pie [S], 14
Tomato prawn cups [W], 14
Tynwald pie [M], 17
Welsh faggots, 12
Winter casserole [B], 29